Notes and Quotes

Jon Connell

Contents

For Alexandra, Ivar, Flora and Ciara, and all my family and friends

Introduction

George Orwell once wrote of an author "no more able to resist a quotation than some people are to refuse a drink". I know what Orwell meant. The temptation – when compiling any miscellany of quotations – is to go on adding to it until it grows into one of those huge tomes no one can bear to open. So, in the spirit of The Week, I've done my best to keep this one short.

It is now 25 years since I founded The Week. I finally left it last year, following its acquisition by a private equity company, but felt I couldn't let such a special anniversary pass without marking it in some way. Our wit and wisdom column has always been popular – my mother used to turn to it first – so I thought I'd bring together a collection of my own favourite quotations, interspersing them with a few longer extracts, the odd anecdote and the occasional piece of poetry. Many of the quotations that appear here once appeared in The Week; others I have collected over the years.

A few years ago, the late Felix Dennis, who never wavered in his support after his enthusiastic early investment in The Week, asked me to do a little book of my editor's letters (*Short and to the point*). At his request, I also wrote a brief introduction about The Week's origins, which I reproduce here. Some of you may have already read it, so it comes at the end as a very dispensable "last word".

A wartime letter

This is an excerpt from a letter written by Evelyn Waugh (while serving with a commando unit) to his wife Laura on 31 May 1942. We came across it in the early days of The Week and thought it might make an unusual addition to the letters page.

Darling...

No. 3 Cmdo were very anxious to be chums with Lord Glasgow so they offered to blow up an old tree stump for him and he was very grateful and he said don't spoil the plantation of young trees near it because that is the apple of my eye and they said no of course not we can blow a tree down so that it falls on a sixpence and Lord Glasgow said goodness you are clever and he asked them all to luncheon for the great explosion. So Col. Durnford-Slater D.S.O. said to his subaltern, have you put enough explosive in the tree. Yes sir, 75 lbs. Is that enough? Yes sir I worked it out by mathematics it is exactly right. Well better put a bit more. Very good sir.

And when Col. D. Slater D.S.O. had had his port he sent for the subaltern and said subaltern better put a bit more explosive in that tree. I don't want to disappoint Lord Glasgow. Very good sir.

Then they all went out to see the explosion and Col.

D.S. D.S.O. said you will see that tree fall flat at just that angle where it will hurt no young trees and Lord Glasgow said goodness you are clever.

So soon they lit the fuse and waited for the explosion and presently the tree, instead of falling quietly sideways, rose 50 feet into the air taking with it half an acre of soil and the whole of the young plantation.

And the subaltern said Sir I made a mistake, it should have been 7.5 lbs not 75.

Lord Glasgow was so upset he walked in dead silence back to his castle and when they came to the turn of the drive in sight of his castle what should they find but that every pane of glass in the building was broken.

So Lord Glasgow gave a little cry and ran to hide his emotion in the lavatory and there when he pulled the plug the entire ceiling, loosened by the explosion, fell on his head.

This is quite true.

Interpreting Shakespeare...

Frank Johnson on how Hamlet might have summarised his problems on the Oprah Winfrey show:

> My mother's married my uncle, only weeks after my father's death. My father's ghost keeps telling me to kill my uncle, but I don't feel like it. Anyway, I've just killed my girlfriend's father. My girlfriend's gone and drowned herself. I think her brother is trying to kill me.

...and D.H. Lawrence

From an anonymous review of *Lady Chatterley's Lover* in the magazine Field and Stream:

> This fictional account of the day-to-day life of an English gamekeeper contains many passages on pheasant raising, apprehension of poachers, ways to control vermin and other chores of the professional gamekeeper. Unfortunately, one is obliged to wade through many pages of extraneous material in order to discover these sidelights. In this reviewer's opinion this book cannot take the place of J. R. Miller's *Practical Gamekeeping*.

Unforeseen consequences

• Michael Kenneally, butler to the Sykes family of Sledmere in Yorkshire, was in the great tradition of eccentric English butlers. When Kenneally died in 1999, it was reported that he liked to let off steam by roaring "Let the buggers wait" as the bell in the dining room rang and rang, and once entered the dining room on a bicycle, cycling round the table with a stack of plates till he overbalanced and crashed to the floor.

Another famous English butler, recalled by David McKie in The Guardian, was kept on by his mistress despite his love of the bottle. One night, however, when a famous statesman came for dinner, he was so incapable that she wrote him a note. "You are drunk and disgusting," it said. "Please leave the room at once." The butler "surveyed it blearily, then shuffled uncertainly to the place where the statesman sat and plonked it down on his plate. "Her ladyship," he mumbled, "asked me to give you this."

• Diarists can see the same event very differently. Describing a dinner party he attended with the comic actor Kenneth Williams, Gyles Brandreth said that Williams had dominated the evening, rarely drawing breath. Williams, however, had clearly been listening as well as talking. In his own account (in his diaries), he notes that another of the diners, Roddy Llewellyn, was a gifted storyteller:

> Roddy told a story about a man going into the home of two spinsters to view a Ming vase and seeing a French letter lying on the piano stool. The old lady explained: "We found it lying on the grass on the common and it said *Place on organ to avoid infection* and we haven't got an organ so we put it on the piano and you know we've neither of us had *any colds* this year!"

• When it was reported (in November 2002) that short-term memory problems might be curable by a drug called Modafinil, the playwright John Mortimer wondered if this might take some of the comic relief out of life. An actor playing his father in the theatre, for example, routinely forgot his lines so had them played into a device fixed to his ear. This worked well enough, until the mechanism somehow got mixed up with a radio taxi service. "At a highly emotional moment of the play, he was heard to say to my mother: 'I am to proceed immediately to number 4 Flask Walk, Hampstead.'" It was, says Mortimer, a moment to be cherished.

Life and how we deal with it

"Mankind faces a crossroads. One path leads to despair and utter hopelessness. The other, to total extinction. Let us pray we have the wisdom to choose correctly."
Woody Allen

"As I looked out into the night sky, across all those infinite stars, it made me realise how unimportant they are."
Peter Cook, comedian

"A secret is something that is only repeated to one person at a time."
Robert McCrum, writer and editor

"Our enemies come nearer the truth in the opinions they form of us than we do in our opinion of ourselves."
Francois de La Rochefoucauld, author

"Thinking is to humans what swimming is to cats – something we can do if absolutely necessary, but we'd really rather not."
Mark Earls, writer and marketing consultant

"Shoes don't stretch and men don't change."
Amy Dalley, American country music singer

"The art of being wise is the art of knowing what to overlook."
William James, American psychologist, brother of novelist Henry James

"Nothing matters very much and very little matters at all."
Arthur Balfour, British PM 1902-1905

"How can I tell what I think until I see what I say."
E.M. Forster, novelist

"Malibu is the only place in the world where you can lie on the sand and look at the stars – or vice versa."
Joan Rivers, comedian

"A bank is a place that will lend you money if you can prove that you don't need it."
Bob Hope, comedian

"The cock may crow but it's the hen who lays the eggs."
Margaret Thatcher

"If I had to live my life all over again, I'd do it exactly the same – only I wouldn't read *Beowulf*."
Woody Allen

"A paranoid is someone who knows a little of what is going on."
William Burroughs, American writer and artist

"My loathings are simple: stupidity, oppression, crime, cruelty, soft music."
Vladimir Nabokov, novelist

"In headaches and in worry vaguely life leaks away."
W. H. Auden

"It would have been splendid... if the wine had been as cold as the soup, the beef as rare as the service, the brandy as old as the fish, and the maid as willing as the duchess."
Winston Churchill on a dinner

"Shyness is just egoism out of its depth."
Penelope Keith, actress

"The great thing to remember is that things aren't as bad as they were in the 14th century."
Tom Holland, historian

"The most certain sign of wisdom is cheerfulness."
Michel de Montaigne, philosopher

Success

"There is no such thing as a great talent without great will power."
Honoré de Balzac, novelist

"You only have to do a very few things right in your life, so long as you don't do too many things wrong."
Warren Buffett, billionaire investor

"Vulnerability is the condition of all achievement."
Terry Eagleton, British literary critic

"In any successful enterprise there must be an uneven number of directors and three is too many."
Giovanni Agnelli, Italian industrialist

"A leader should be light-hearted and full of hope, by means of his facial expression, his words and his dress."
Marshal Montecuccoli, 17th century, Italian-born soldier and strategist

"The most difficult thing is the decision to act; the rest is merely tenacity."
Amelia Earhart, first woman to fly solo across the Atlantic

"There's no limit to what a man might accomplish if he doesn't mind who takes the credit."
Ronald Reagan

"The heights that great men reached and kept
Were not attained by sudden flight,
But they, while their companions slept,
Were toiling upward in the night."
Longellow, from The Ladder of St Augustine (1858)

"Most successes are unhappy. That's why they are successes – they have to reassure themselves by achieving something that the world will notice."
Agatha Christie

"All men are mad who devote themselves to the pursuit of power when they can be fishing or painting pictures, or sitting in the sun."
A. J. P. Taylor, historian

"Concentration comes out of a combination of confidence and hunger."
Arnold Palmer, golfer

"Goodness you've done well," the actress **Mae West** was once told. "Goodness had nothing to do with it," she replied.

Two verses

I came across the first of these two verses, by **Wordsworth**, a few days after thinking up The Week, and found it rather inspiring. The second, by **Elizabeth Coleridge**, was a favourite of the late W. F. Deedes.

> Enough, if something from our hands have power
> To live, and act, and serve the future hour;
> And if, as toward the silent tomb we go,
> Through love, through hope, and faith's
> transcendent dower,
> We feel that we are greater than we know.
> *From Sonnets from the River Duddon: After-Thought*

> But the dreams their children dreamed
> Fleeting, unsubstantial, vain,
> Shadowy as the shadows seemed,
> Airy nothing, as they deemed,
> These remain.
> *From Egypt's Might Is Tumbled Down*

Advice

"When you have exhausted all the possibilities, remember this – you haven't."
Thomas Edison, American inventor

"The difference between successful people and really successful people is that really successful people say no to almost everything."
Warren Buffett

"It is a very funny thing about life: if you refuse to accept anything but the best, you very often get it."
W. Somerset Maugham, playwright and novelist

"Men must be either pampered or crushed, because they can get revenge for small injuries but not for grievous ones."
Niccolo Machiavelli, Italian diplomat

"Smile. Tomorrow will be worse."
Woody Allen

"Do remember to place your candles in the fridge for two or three hours before use, or they could burn unevenly."
Guide for training navy cooks, quoted in The Guardian

"Always be sincere, even if you don't mean it."
Harry Truman, US president 1945-1953

"Attention is the rarest and purest form of generosity."
Simone Weil, French philosopher

"Give people the chance to say 'no' to you. If they say it enough, they will feel beholden to you to come back with a 'yes' by way of compensation."
Hilary Rubin, American author

"Everything looks better after lunch."
Winston Churchill

"A good leader is someone who takes a little more than his share of the blame and a little less than his share of the credit."
John C. Maxwell, American author

"If you would stand well with a great mind, leave him with a favourable impression of yourself; if with a little mind, with a favourable impression of himself."
Samuel Taylor Coleridge, poet

"The one thing I have learned over the years is the difference between taking one's work seriously and one's self seriously. The first is imperative and the second is disastrous."
Margot Fonteyn, ballerina

"Easy writing makes hard reading. I'm not a writer. I'm a rewriter. Write so that it springs along."
Clive James, critic and journalist

"Whether you think that you can, or that you can't, you are usually right."
Henry Ford, industrialist

"Never write when you can speak. Never speak when you can nod."
Martin Lomasney, legendary Boston politician

"Talk low, talk slow and don't say much."
John Wayne

"Progress isn't made by early risers. It's made by lazy men trying to find easier ways to do something."
Robert Heinlein, Science Fiction writer

"If you're going to do something, go start. Life's simpler than we sometimes can admit."
Robert De Niro

"Nothing gives one person so great an advantage over another, as to remain always cool and unruffled under all circumstances."
Thomas Jefferson, US president 1801-1809

"...there is nothing either good or bad, but thinking makes it so."
Shakespeare, *Hamlet*

"As a rule, there is no surer way to the dislike of men than to behave well where they have behaved badly."
Lew Wallace, US lawyer and Union general in the American Civil War

"My grandmother told me to find something nice to say about everyone and say it."
Jilly Cooper, author (to Hunter Davies)

"Several excuses are always less convincing than one."
Aldous Huxley, novelist and philosopher

"At my school we were taught that silence was the unbearable riposte."
Sir Alec Douglas Home, British PM 1963-1964

"If at first you don't succeed, try, try again. Then quit. No use being a damn fool about it."
W. C. Fields, comedian

"Use advisers carefully... Above all don't ask them for advice."
Hugh Osmond, British businessman

"I have found the best way to give advice to your children is to find out what they want and then advise them to do it."
Harry Truman

"When choosing between two evils I always like to try the one I've never tried before."
Mae West, American actress

"Three things in life are important: the first is to be kind; the second is to be kind; and the third is to be kind."
Henry James

"The minute you settle for less than you deserve, you get even less than you settled for."
Maureen Dowd, New York Times columnist

"Sit as little as possible, and give no credence to any thought that was not born outdoors."
Nietzsche

- "Pretend you're telling the story to your mother, or to a friend in the pub."

Advice given to me when I was a trainee journalist doing a four-month course at the Thomson Training Scheme in Newcastle in late 1975.

***

- "The secret of controlling other people is to let them do the talking."

"Always believe you can hole a putt – even if it's from the edge of the green."

Two pieces of advice from my first editor, Peter Watson, in 1976. He was the editor of The Press and Journal in Aberdeen and a very good golfer.

***

- "It's worth remembering this: if you're nice to people sometimes they're nice back to you."

The main piece of advice Frank Giles gave me when, as the then editor of The Sunday Times, he sent me to Washington in 1983.

Literary critics

This is extracted from what was originally a diary piece written for the Telegraph magazine in 2017. I had set up Connell Guides – to publish short literary guides on classic texts – a few years before that. We now have more than 80, covering history as well as English literature.

I also have a new All You Need to Know series of books which I was preparing to launch when this diary was written.

Among the pleasures of editing my little English literature guides is being reminded of how staggeringly rude novelists can be about each other. "One of the worst, weakest, least sane, most *voulu* (i.e. forced) books I have ever read," wrote Robert Louis Stephenson to Henry James about *Tess of the d'Urbervilles*. "Oh yes, dear Louis, she is vile," agreed James. "The pretence of sexuality is only equalled by the absence of it." "A narrow-guttted spinster," said D. H. Lawrence of Jane Austen. How cross he would be to find no one reads him any more while she's as popular as ever.

Mark Twain would be cross too: "any library is a good library if it has no book by Jane Austen in it," he said. It was a shame she'd died peacefully, Twain thought. "Every time I read *Pride and Prejudice* I long to dig her up and beat her over the skull with her own shin-bone." (The "every time" is interesting. Why keep re-reading a book you hate so much?)

It's one thing to be rude about an individual novelist; quite another to dismiss a whole literary tradition. In his 1960s book, *Love and Death in the American Novel*, the brave New York critic Leslie Fiedler, argues that most American classics are essentially infantile; it is no accident, he says, that they are usually to be found not just on children's but on boys' bookshelves. "The mythic America is boyhood." Where, he wondered, was the American equivalent of grown-up books about women like *Pride and Prejudice* or *Anna Karenina* or *Madame Bovary*? (Henry James, he thought, belonged more to the European literary tradition.)

Unlike Twain's blast at Austen there is much to be said for the Fiedler view: while there are notable exceptions – like Edith Wharton – many of the best American novels – e.g. *Moby Dick, Huckleberry Finn, Catcher in the Rye, To Kill a Mockingbird*, and indeed *The Great Gatsby* – are essentially "buddy novels", about the relationship between men or men and boys rather than between men and women. Needless to say, Fiedler's book was greeted with howls of outrage from his fellow critics.

***

My new series of short books is aimed at time-pressed autodidacts, people who want to learn but find the prospect of reading 700 pages daunting. So how to promote them? I visited schools with the guides to spread the word, and once went to beautiful Bradfield College, near Reading, to address a small group of Heads of English. On the grounds that showing beats telling I brought along a suitcase full of guides to impress them with.

Standing up to speak, I heaved the suitcase on to the table. But when I opened it, I was shocked, indeed amazed, to find that it contained not books but an assortment of women's clothing – knickers, bras, shirts, trainers. Somehow I'd managed to leave the train at Reading not with my own suitcase but with someone else's – one which looked identical. Whether my unfortunate fellow passenger ever retrieved her clothes from Left Luggage at Paddington I never discovered – but I owe her a debt. The teachers present still talk about the occasion. It was an effective piece of marketing but sadly not a trick I can repeat.

Writers on writing

"Happy endings depend entirely on stopping the story before it's over."
Orson Welles

"The great Russian novels of the 19th century arise from the failure of a class, whereas the English spring out of its success."
V. S. Pritchett

"Do I believe it? Do I care? Will I go on caring?"
Philip Larkin's three criteria for a good novel

"Books say: she did this because. Life says: she did this. Books are where things are explained to you; life is where they aren't."
Julian Barnes

"The truth is that the greatness of English literature for most of this century resides not in adult novels but in writing for children. I genuinely think that Roald Dahl is a greater writer than Martin Amis."
Melanie McDonagh

"To write a good novel you have to know a lot and have thought about things."
Kingsley Amis – though I'm quoting from memory

"I think you will find that the sun is always shining in my books – a state of affairs which minutely lifts the spirit of the English reader."
Ian Fleming

"Novels today are all about women being sad in Fulham."
Kingsley Amis

"They loved in triangles and lived in squares."
Dorothy Parker on the Bloomsbury group

"Every writer knows that the crucial part of his work is neither logical nor random, but the fruit of a mysterious process which we call, for want of a better word, 'inspiration'. The best jokes, the most tear-jerking moments, the intellectually satisfying twists simply *come*; they drift into the mind, amusing and moving the surprised author no less than his reader."
Anthony Lejeune in a letter to The Daily Telegraph

"It's like a strain on the eyesight. I find that I have to know — even if I'm not writing it — where my character's sitting, what his movements are. It's this focusing, even though it's not focusing on the page, that strains my eyes, as though I were watching something too close."
Graham Greene

Joseph Conrad also said his eyes got tired first when writing. His aim was "by the power of the written word, to make you hear, to make you feel – it is, before all, to make you see".

"I knew one thing about each of my characters which I never told the reader."
Arthur Ransome

"Make 'em cry, make 'em laugh, make 'em wait."
Wilkie Collins

"Don't tell me the moon is shining. Show me the glint of light on broken glass."
Anton Chekhov

"Childhood is the bank balance of the writer."
Graham Greene

National stereotypes die hard, as some of the quotes in the next five pages remind us...

Europe

"I take care to travel only on Italian ships because, in the event of disaster, there is none of that nonsense about women and children first."
Noel Coward, playwright and director

The EEC is a horse and carriage. Germany is the horse, France the coachman."
Charles de Gaulle, president of France, 1959-69

"One could hardly think of a worse name than the Euro. Two-syllable words ending with 'o' do not generally inspire confidence – weirdo, psycho, Rambo, porno, pseudo, gringo and bingo."
Quentin Crewe in the London Magazine (1996)

The French

"When God created France he found it so perfect that, to comfort those who couldn't live there, he invented the French."
Old saying

"The English fondness for France is normally a sort of neutron love: take away the people and leave the buildings standing."
Anthony Lane in The New Yorker

"Europe was set up by clever, Catholic, left-wing, French bureaucrats. Most Brits have a problem with at least three of those five."
Peter Hennessy, historian

"The French, unlike – and this cannot be said often enough, the Germans – hate the English. They hate us because in war we have never been defeated. While they, since the battle of Leipzig in 1813, have never been victorious."
Alan Clarke, MP, author and diarist

The English

"Curse... the blasted, jelly-boned swines, the snivelling, dribbling, dithering, palsied, pulse-less lot that make up England today. God, how I hate them! Why, why, why was I born an Englishman?"
D. H. Lawrence in a letter to Edward Garnett in 1912

"The insularity of the English, their refusal to take foreigners seriously, is a folly that has to be paid

for very heavily from time to time."
George Orwell

"Here is a country that fought and won a noble war, dismantled a mighty empire in a generally benign and enlightened way, created a far-seeing welfare state – in short, did nearly everything right – and then spent the rest of the century looking on itself as a chronic failure. The fact is that this is still the best place in the world for most things – to post a letter, go for a walk, watch television, buy a book, venture out for a drink, go to a museum, use the bank, get lost, seek help, or stand on a hillside and take in a view."
Bill Bryson, *Notes on a Small Island*, 1995

"The comfortably off ought always to bear in mind G. K. Chesterton's remark that the agreeable character of English life 'does not rest on the kindness of the rich to the poor. It rests on the perennial and unfailing kindness of the poor to the rich.'"
Ferdinand Mount, British author and novelist

Union leaders

"Union leaders are remarkably even-tempered men – always angry."
Max Hastings, historian and journalist

The Welsh (and young people)

"If there's one thing I hate more than the Welsh, it's the young. I hate young people with a passion. I wish them all ill. People under the age of 40 don't see anything. Even if they do, they don't really know what they are seeing."
Dennis Potter, TV dramatist

Etonians

"At Eton, you are trained not to talk about feelings, to be narrow-minded and to employ people who went to Winchester."
Henry Cole, film director

"He was educated at Eton and at Oxford, so Watson, bring the gun."
Sherlock Holmes

Americans

"I dislike America and on the whole, though there are many exceptions to this, I dislike Americans. I find them as I find the English abroad: noisy and exceptionally ignorant about the world."
Graham Greene

To the comment: "You'll have the vote of every thinking American!" **Adlai Stevenson** replied: "That's not enough, I need a majority."

"On some great and glorious day, the plain folks of the land will reach their heart's desire at last, and the White House will be adorned with a moron." **H. L. Mencken, essayist and critic**

"Be nice to America – or we'll bring you democracy." **US bumper sticker after the invasion of Iraq**

Lawyers

"Lawyers: people who write a 10,000-word document and then call it a brief." **Franz Kafka**

Pheasant shooting

"Up flies £10, bang goes 10p and down falls £1." **The economics of pheasant shooting, as explained to Edward Garnier MP by his uncle**

Luck

There are four principles of luck, says **Professor Richard Wiseman** (in *The Luck Factor*):

"Lucky people are skilled at creating and noticing chance opportunities; make lucky decisions by listening to their intuition; create self-fulfilling prophecies via positive expectations; and adopt a resilient attitude that transforms bad luck into good."

"You never know what worse luck your bad luck has saved you from."
Cormac McCarthy, American novelist

Other people

"Whatever you may be sure of, be sure of this: that you are dreadfully like other people."
James Russell Lowell, US poet and critic

"You can tell more about a person by what he says about others than you can by what others say about him."
Audrey Hepburn

"Some cause happiness wherever they go; others whenever they go."
Oscar Wilde

"You will become way less concerned what other people think of you when you realise how seldom they do."
David Foster Wallace, American writer and professor

"Women dress alike all over the world. They dress to be annoying to other women."
Elsa Schiaparelli, Italian fashion designer

"Hell is other people at breakfast."
Jean-Paul Sartre, philosopher

"What you say about somebody else, anybody else, reveals you."
James Baldwin, US novelist and playwright

"Most people are other people. Their thoughts are someone else's opinions, their life a mimicry, their passions a quotation."
Oscar Wilde

"Among those whom I like or admire, I can find no common denominator, but among those whom I love, I can: all of them make me laugh."
W. H. Auden

"You must come again when you have less time,"
Painter Walter Sickert to a departing guest

"A bore is a man who, when you ask him how he is, tells you."
Bert Leston Taylor, American journalist

"A great many people think they are thinking, when they are merely rearranging their prejudices."
William James, psychologist, brother of novelist Henry James

"Imagining what it is like to be someone other than yourself is at the core of our humanity. It is the essence of compassion, and the beginning of morality."
Ian McEwan, novelist

"Other people, as we get to know them, are like strips of metal dipped in acid: they gradually lose their good qualities – and their defects too, at times."
Marcel Proust

"Sister Helen Loder was cycling through her parish when a boy shouted at her, 'F***** nun'. She dismounted from her bicycle and said: 'One or the other, but I can't be both.'"
Quoted by A. N. Wilson in the Evening Standard

"Charm is the ability to be truly interested in other people."
Richard Avedon, American photographer

"Oppression is what they do in the West. What they do in the Middle East is their 'culture'."
Robert Harris, novelist

"The life of a person is not what happened, but what he remembers and how he remembers it."
Gabriel Garcia Marquez

Posterity

"All civilisation might be defined as an attempt to give meaning to death."
Roger Scruton, philosopher

"Lives of great men remind us
We can make our lives sublime
And departing leave behind us
Footprints on the sands of time."
Longfellow, from A Psalm of Life (1838)

"To sail beyond the sunset, and the baths
Of all the western stars, until I die.
It may be that the gulfs will wash us down:
It may be we shall touch the Happy Isles,
And see the great Achilles, whom we knew.
Tho' much is taken, much abides; and tho'
We are not now that strength which in old days
Moved earth and heaven, that which we are, we are;
One equal temper of heroic hearts,
Made weak by time and fate, but strong in will
To strive, to seek, to find, and not to yield."
Tennyson, from Ulysses

Conversation

"No one really listens to anyone else, and if you try
it for a while you'll see why."
Mignon McLaughlin, American journalist

"There is no such thing as conversation. There are
intersecting monologues, that is all."
Rebecca West, novelist

"A professor is one who talks in someone else's
sleep."
W. H. Auden

The importance of novels

"The novel, as D.H. Lawrence said, is 'the bright book of life'. It does the human condition better than any other art form. If you want to know about people, about societies or cultures, the thing to do is read a novel, not read a work of history or a work of academic commentary. Novels are the best route to understanding the curious people we are, and the curious adventure we're all embarked on."
William Boyd (talking to me for Connell Guides)

"What good novels do is take you deep inside the psychological processes, the personalities and the experiences of other people which would not otherwise be available to you. If you think about talking with your friends, it's not often that you really get the chance to have them really explain their life from the inside out to you. There isn't time in the day, you wouldn't know how to ask the question anyway, they might not wish to tell you and they might not have the words with which to tell you. As a child I learnt more from reading books than I did from other people. I find it hard to understand how people who haven't read Austen, Dickens, D. H. Lawrence etc know what other people think and feel."
Sebastian Faulks (as above)

An Irish story

Spotted on a loo wall in the Cobblers Cove hotel in Barbados:

The Confession

"Bless me father for I have sinned. I have been with a loose woman."
"Is that you, little Tommy Shaughnessy?"
"Yes Father, it is."
"And who was the woman you were with?"
"Sure and I can't be telling you, Father. I don't want to ruin her reputation."
"Well Tommy, I'll find out sooner or later so you may as well be telling me now. Was it Brenda O'Malley?"
"I cannot say."
"Was it Patricia Kelly?"
"I'll never tell."
"Was it Liz Shannon?"
"Please Father, I cannot tell you."
The priest sighs. "You're a steadfast lad, Tommy, and I admire that. But you've sinned and you must atone. You cannot attend church for three months. Be off with you now."
Tommy walks back to his pew. His friend Sean slides over and asks: "What did you get?"
"Three months vacation and three good leads," says Tommy.

Happiness

"Very happy people invariably like themselves."
Graham Turner in the Daily Mail

"One of the secrets of a happy life is continuous small treats."
Iris Murdoch, novelist

"The recipe for a happy life is a good digestion and a bad memory."
Ingrid Bergman, actress

"To be without some of the things you want is an indispensable part of happiness."
Bertrand Russell, philosopher

"A lifetime of happiness? No man could bear it."
George Bernard Shaw

"Happiness isn't something you experience; it's something you remember."
Oscar Levant, concert pianist and composer

"The happiest part of a man's life is what he passes lying awake in bed in the morning."
Dr Johnson

"If one can't be happy one must be amused, don't you agree?"
Nancy Mitford, novelist

"To be happy, we must not be too concerned with others."
Albert Camus, philosopher

"Happiness is a how, not a what; a talent, not an object."
Hermann Hesse, poet and novelist

"I have learned that everyone wants to live on the peak of the mountain, without knowing that the real happiness is in how it is scaled."
Gabriel Garcia Marquez, Colombian novelist

"To be happy you have to value little things, to be good at ordinariness... to value dullness, to savour details, the textures of things...."
Joanna Trollope, novelist

"One is never as unhappy as one thinks, nor as happy as one hopes."
La Rochefoucauld

"We don't realise how quickly we will adapt to a pleasurable event and make it the backdrop of our lives. When any event occurs to us, we make it ordinary. And through [it] becoming ordinary, we lose our pleasure."
Tim Wilson, American psychologist

"Oscar Hammerstein [the lyricist] said that what moved him to tears was not tragedy but sudden happiness."
Anthony Lejeune in The Daily Telegraph

"Puritanism... the haunting fear that someone, somewhere, may be happy."
H. L. Mencken

"Happiness is an imaginary condition, formerly attributed by the living to the dead, now usually attributed by adults to children, and by children to adults."
Thomas Szasz, pscyhiatrist

"Thank heavens, the sun has gone in and I don't have to go out and enjoy it."
Logan Pearsall Smith, essayist

Politics and politicians

"The trouble with socialism is that it would take too many evenings."
Beatrice Webb, English socialist and historian

"I asked Boris Yeltsin to tell me briefly what the situation in Russia was like. "Good," he said. I asked for a longer version. "Not good," he replied."
John Major

"When I left the dining room after sitting next to Mr. Gladstone, I thought he was the cleverest man in England. But after sitting next to Mr. Disraeli, I thought I was the cleverest woman in England."
Unknown but sometimes attributed to **Jenny Jerome, Winston Churchill's mother.**

"There's a lot to be said for that chappie. Much smarter than you think he is. And always reliable. Don't think he has an enemy in the world. It's a great pity the Labour Party doesn't have that kind of person to call upon."
Harold Wilson *on his predecessor as prime minister, Alec Douglas Home. (When Wilson took over as prime minister he asked Douglas Home to maintain a scrambler telephone at The Hirsel, his house in Scotland, so he, Wilson, could "seek guidance".)*

"When I came to the Treasury, they predicted to me that I would become the most unpopular man in Britain. This was the only correct forecast the Treasury made in the several years I was chancellor."
Norman Lamont, former UK chancellor

"God help the Tory party if the Tories ever get hold of it."
Matthew Parris in The Spectator

"Far better not."
Habitual response of **Lord Hartington**, *who held several Cabinet posts, whenever any proposal or scheme was put to him.*

"Labour stands for envy and hope, the Conservatives for nostalgia and fear."
William Cooper, English novelist

"I have orders to be awakened at any time in case of a national emergency, even if I'm in a cabinet meeting."
Ronald Reagan

"The trouble with socialism is socialism – but the trouble with capitalism is capitalists."
Willi Schlamm, Austrian-American journalist

"The difference between a welfare state and a totalitarian state is a matter of time."
Ayn Rand, Russian-American writer and philosopher

"Under capitalism, man exploits man, while under communism it's the other way round."
Old Czech joke

"Communism is the longest path from capitalism to capitalism."
Old Russian joke

"And so while the great ones depart to their dinner
the secretary stays, getting thinner and thinner,
racking his brains to record and report
what he thinks that they think they ought to
                                        have thought."
Arthur Bryant, historian

"The best argument against democracy is a five-
minute conversation with the average voter."
Winston Churchill

"Overseas aid is a transfer of money from poor
people in rich countries to rich people in poor
countries."
**Peter Bauer, Hungarian-born British
economist**

"One of life's abiding ironies is that people inclined
towards ideological selfishness are often selflessly
heroic towards individuals in need, whereas
liberals talk a good game but don't always show up
in a crisis."
Decca Aitkenhead in The Times

Three stories about Margaret Thatcher

• Once Mrs Thatcher compared something at a meeting to Waiting for Godot, pronouncing Godot with a hard t. Lord Carrington, then her Foreign Secretary, whispered: "It's pronounced Godo, Prime Minister." "How's it spelt?" Carrington spelt it out. "Then it's Godot," said Mrs Thatcher, pronouncing the hard t with even more emphasis. **From Charles Moore's biography of Margaret Thatcher**

• When Chris Patten was governor of Hong Kong, only one of his guests would always make the bed in the mornings: Mrs Thatcher. "My wife once crept in to see how well she'd done it and it looked as though a sergeant major had been in to do it."

• "I hear that John Major [the prime minister], in spite of professing to be the simple man, has a yearning for grandeur. He has police outriders, which Mrs Thatcher never had. And he is now to get a powerful official plane. Mrs Thatcher never minded what sort of plane she had; but if it went too fast, she would certainly see that it reduced its cruising speed in order to save petrol." **From the diaries of royal biographer Kenneth Rose (May 30, 1992)**

Lunch with Kenneth Clarke

One Monday, while he was Chancellor, Ken Clarke arrived for lunch with Max Hastings, then editor of the Evening Standard. "I had trouble finding anywhere to park." "Surely you've got a driver." "Oh, it's been a hell of a day. My car wouldn't start at home in Nottingham, and in the end I drove myself straight here." "Couldn't you have rung the office on a mobile?" "Never switch it on. I like to listen to a bit of jazz on the M1." After lunch, when Clarke went off to find his meter, Hastings found desperate messages on his own car phone, urging the Chancellor to call the Treasury.

Religion

"Nothing returns one quicker to God than the sight of a scientist with no imagination, no vocabulary, no sympathy, no comprehension of metaphor, and no wit, looking soulless and forlorn amid the wonders of nature."
Howard Jacobson, novelist, on Richard Dawkins, author and outspoken atheist

"Atheism is a crutch for those who can't bear the reality of God."
Tom Stoppard, playwright

"I don't want to miss out on heaven due to a technicality."
Elvis Presley on why he wore a cross, a star of David and the Hebrew letter chai

"I don't believe in God, but I miss him."
Julian Barnes, novelist

"If it turns out that there is a God, I don't think that he's evil. But the worst that you can say about him is that basically he's an underachiever."
Woody Allen

Christianity

"[At] the age of about 18, when I left the town for university, I also left the Church. It was not as abrupt as it sounds, but at university I experienced the common delusion that only reason mattered... I am still unable to cross the River of Jordan which would lead me to the crucial belief in a godly eternity. But that early faith, powerfully held, is no more capable of being erased than the memory of the first real love affair and it is part of me still...

"I wrote my book [on the King James Bible] because I was first irritated and then appalled at the way [the Bible's] profound and often beneficial effect on humanity across so many areas has been

rubbed out of our history... Like no other nation, we had a national book and it was the King James Bible... Einstein wrote that he was a 'believing unbeliever'. Stephen Hawking speaks of worlds of thought which we shall never know... I think most of us sense that now and then we have pulses from it – in passion, in daydreams, 'surprised by joy'. I respect those who have no faith or little faith or are indifferent to it, but the current notion that atheistic reason marks the apotheosis of human intelligence, strikes me as being very doubtful. I'm as certain as I can be that there's more to come."
Melvyn Bragg, writing in The Daily Telegraph, June 2011

***

"[*Macbeth* is a play] fed at its sources by the ethics of Jesus. For the creating mind that fuses imaginative identification *with* Macbeth and a moral judgement on Macbeth, into a single act of dramatic recognition, is one which has grown accustomed to stretching itself Christianly between trenchant judgement and wise suspension of judgement.

"Its poise and assurance is supported by the Christianity it has breathed from its earliest years. Which does not necessarily mean that Shakespeare was a 'believer' in the conventional sense – George Eliot in *Middlemarch* seems to have drawn a similar strength from a Christianity she rejected – but that he was supported in a thousand indefinable ways in the Christian climate in which he lived. He could take these things for granted, did not need to be noisily assertive about them, could rest in them." **Wilbur Sanders, *The Dramatist and the Received Idea*, quoted in the Connell Guide to *Macbeth* by Graham Bradshaw**

***

"The message of [George Orwell's *1984*] is very bleak. The most shrewd criticism of the book came from Evelyn Waugh. They had a very unlikely friendship at the end of Orwell's life – because he was in a sanatorium near where Waugh lived, Waugh visited him and Orwell gave him a copy of *1984*. Waugh wrote [to Orwell] saying: 'It's a very powerful book, but you've made one mistake in my opinion. You have underestimated the power of religious faith.'

"There is no Christianity, no religious faith and no church in *1984*, and Waugh, writing before Solidarity and before the Polish pope, put his finger on the weakness of the book. It's reductive, it's Marxist, it doesn't allow space for faith. Religion is the one element that's missing from *1984*, and I think that is a legitimate criticism of it." **Robert Harris (talking to me for Connell Guides)**

Music

"Those who have never heard it for themselves may recreate it in the comfort and privacy of their own homes by setting fire to the tail of their pet cat."
Craig Brown on Yoko Ono's song, Don't Worry Kyoko (Mummy's Only Putting Her Hand in the Snow), Evening Standard

"[John] once arrived at a recording studio with a song for A Hard Day's Night, their new film. The tune was in his head and the words were on a birthday card sent by a fan to his son... The song went: *But when I get home to you/ I find my tiredness is through/ And I feel all right...* I said I thought 'My tiredness is through' was a weak line. 'Ok," he said cheerfully, and getting out his pen, crossed it out and wrote: *I find the things that you do/ Will make me feel all right.*
Maureen Cleave on John Lennon

"Someone said to me, 'But the Beatles were anti-materialistic.' That's a huge myth. John and I literally used to sit down and say, 'Now, let's write a swimming pool.'"
Paul McCartney

Fan: "You don't know who I am, but I know who you are." **Bob Dylan**: "Let's keep it that way."

Shakespeare and Shaw

"My own view is that probably none of the plays were written by Shakespeare, but by someone of the same name."
Frank Johnson, journalist

George Bernard Shaw: "I am enclosing two tickets to the first night of my new play. Bring a friend... if you have one."
Winston Churchill: "Cannot possibly attend first night, will attend second... if there is one."

Art, drama and poetry

"The purpose of art is washing the dust of daily life off our souls."
Pablo Picasso

"We make art from the quarrel with ourselves, mere rhetoric from the quarrel with others."
W. B. Yeats

"David Lean [the film director] proved the old theory that great artists are closer to bad art than are good artists. Where talent is judicious, genius is reckless."
Nigel Andrews in the FT

"We go to poetry, we go to literature in general, to be forwarded within ourselves."
Seamus Heaney, poet

"Art lives from constraints and dies from freedom."
Leonardo da Vinci

The writer **Ferdinand Mount** has made a similar point about great novels [in the TLS]. Novelists, he believes, struggle nowadays because of the disappearance of the old imperial values of restraint and self-sacrifice – what he calls *romanitas*. "Is it possible that writers actually needed *romanitas* as a great flawed project to grate against, as something that generated tragedies and ironies that were worth dealing with, and that without *romanitas* life seems to have less to it?"

Money

"I'm living so far beyond my income that we might almost be said to be living apart."
E. E. Cummings, American poet

"Everyone is always in favour of general economy and particular expenditure."
Anthony Eden, British PM 1955-1957

"I'm tired of love; I'm still more tired of rhyme;
but money gives me pleasure all the time."
Hilaire Belloc, writer and satirist

"Money – the one thing that keeps us in touch
with our children."
Gyles Brandreth, writer and broadcaster

"The idea that money doesn't buy happiness is a
lie put about by the rich, to stop the poor from
killing them."
Michael Caine, actor

"Anyone who says money can't buy you happiness
doesn't know where to shop."
Joan Collins, actress

"Too many people spend money they don't have
on things they don't want to impress people they
don't like."
Will Rogers, American actor

"There are three types of economist: those who
can count and those who can't."
**Eddie George, Governor of the Bank of
England, 1993-2003**

"The best way to make money is to start a
religion."
Ron Hubbard, founder of Scientology

Love and marriage

"What do you mean how many husbands have I had? You mean apart from my own?"
Zsa Zsa Gabor, Hungarian-American actress

"It doesn't matter much whom you marry because it always turns out to be someone else."
Old adage

"They say before a man is married he is incomplete, but after he's married he's finished."
Zsa Zsa Gabor

"I am a marvelous housekeeper. Every time I leave a man, I keep his house."
Zsa Zsa Gabor

"My first wife drove me to drink. It's the only thing I'm indebted to her for."
W. C. Fields

"We had a lot in common. I loved him and he loved him."
Actress Shelley Winters on her ex-husband

"Bigamy is having one wife too many. Monogamy is the same"
Oscar Wilde

"The critical period in matrimony is breakfast time."
A. P. Herbert

"My wife and I were happy for 20 years. Then we met."
Rodney Dangerfield, Edmonton Journal

"When we let romance go, we change the sky for the ceiling."
George Meredith, English novelist

"Sex is totally ludicrous to everybody except the participants."
Alan Plater, playwright and screenwriter

"A kiss is an application on the top floor for a job in the basement."
Artwork at Spectrum Art Exhibition

"Like everything which is not the involuntary result of fleeting emotion but the creation of time and will, any marriage, happy or unhappy, is infinitely more interesting than any romance, however passionate."
W. H. Auden

"So, we'll go no more a roving
So late into the night,
Though the heart be still as loving,
And the moon be still as bright."
Lord Byron

"Love, like sleep, should be approached gently."
The late **Patrick Leigh Fermor** quoted this to me,
though he wasn't sure of the source. Yeats
expresses a similar sentiment in this beautiful if
melancholy poem:

Down by the salley gardens
my love and I did meet;
She passed the salley gardens
with little snow-white feet.
She bid me take love easy,
as the leaves grow on the tree;
But I, being young and foolish,
with her would not agree.

In a field by the river
my love and I did stand,
And on my leaning shoulder
she laid her snow-white hand.
She bid me take life easy,
as the grass grows on the weirs;
But I was young and foolish,
and now am full of tears.
W. B. Yeats

I'll love you, dear, I'll love you,
Till China and Africa meet,
Till the river jumps over the mountain,
And the salmon sing in the street.

I'll love you till the oceans
Are folded and hung out to dry
And the seven seas go squawking,
Like geese about the sky.
W. H. Auden

By the time you swear you're his,
Shivering and sighing.
And he vows his passion is,
Infinite, undying.
Lady make note of this –
One of you is lying.
Dorothy Parker

Founding The Week

The first copy of The Week appeared at 3am on May 10th, 1995. Standing in a huge, brightly lit shed in Bicester, I watched it come sliding down the printing press and picked it up nervously. What if the pages were in the wrong order? What if the pictures were in the wrong place or upside down or missing? What if it was all a hideous mess?

It wasn't. On that score, at least, I needn't have worried. One photograph was missing but at first glance there were no other obvious howlers. To my eyes, it looked just as it should. I felt absurdly pleased with it, and myself. Hours before, these pages had only been images on a computer screen; now here they were, ink on paper, crisp to the touch, a proper magazine at last. Suddenly the publication I'd spent so many hours thinking about was real. It actually existed.

But nice as it was to see a pile of Weeks growing in the corner, this was the easy bit. I'd gone charging into the highly competitive magazine world underfunded, understaffed, with the flimsiest of business plans, zero business experience and almost zero knowledge of my market. Foolhardy didn't begin to describe it.

I'd produced the magazine. Now I needed to produce buyers. So, after a few hours sleep in a local pub, I set out to find some. My first attempt involved driving to the Cobden Club in south west London with a car full of magazines. I'd asked as many people as I could think of who might be prepared to give up a morning to come along with their address books, and when I arrived I offered them a drink and a sandwich, and asked them to mail out copies to people they knew. Kindly, they did.

By mid afternoon more than 1,000 copies of The Week were winging their way with hand-written notes to great aunts and rural solicitors and friends of friends who, I hoped, would all be incredibly grateful to receive this life-changing magazine. Well it's a start, I thought: that will give us a couple of hundred subscribers at least. This turned out to be a wildly optimistic guess. I can't remember how many people we actually signed up from this particular effort but it was probably less than 30.

Despite the best efforts of my friends, most early recipients of The Week must have taken one look at the first subscription price (£67) and thought: you're joking.

"I'd give it ten," said a newspaper circulation manager to a friend of mine. "What – ten out of ten?" replied my friend, rather chuffed.

"No, ten issues."

It was lesson one in my crash course in magazine marketing. In the weeks to come I did everything I could to woo new subscribers. Sir Antony Jay and Joanna Trollope gallantly agreed to say nice things about the magazine and I slapped their quotes on the cover to show potential buyers what good company they'd be keeping. *It wasn't all bad* featured a string of pretty scantily clad women on the grounds that pictures of pretty girls cheer everyone up, men and women, even Guardian readers. I promised potential subscribers that if they signed up they'd be invited to a launch party in London which there was never the slightest prospect of our being able to afford.

Every Thursday, back in the country after publication day, 1 would drive off to the local post office in Devizes, buy lots of stamps and envelopes and send out another 100 or so copies to anyone I could think of. When we moved to a new office in Westbourne Grove soon after launch I hired a Feng Shui consultant to advise on the best layout for success and acquired a money plant – still on my desk, and still alive – in the confident belief it would

---

STARTING A SMALL BUSINESS

Michael Masterson, a Florida businessman who helped us a bit with MoneyWeek, writes well about the qualities an entrepreneur needs in his aptly entitled *Ready, Fire, Aim*. He lists what he calls the five "magic wands" needed to create and develop any successful new business:

• Coming up with good ideas
• Selling products
• Creating the right process for managing a business
• Developing superstars
• Taking action

I agree with all Michael Masterson's points, especially

help us make money.

Well, it couldn't hurt.

Word of mouth soon became, as it has remained, our best marketing tool, but it took a lot longer than I'd hoped, or budgeted for, to get the momentum going. Like many another niche product, The Week was a *success d'estime* long before it made any money.

I included an editor's letter in the early issues to establish our credibility, to explain what we were trying to do and who we were. But the editor's letter was and has remained more than that. It was aimed at giving the magazine a personal touch, to emphasize that The Week was not some sort of computer regurgitating story after story, but a magazine with a slightly idiosyncratic personal view of the world reflected in my letter and the

---

the last one. He writes: "I can't tell you how many times I've seen exciting ideas for new business and product ideas eventually die on the development vine while the people who championed them try to fix every potential problem they – or anyone else they talked to – could think of."

Successful people *always* move ahead quickly with good but imperfect products. Bill Gates didn't worry about bugs. He pushed new Microsoft software out to the public as fast as he could *then* fixed the bugs. Apple, too, goes for good not perfect. Hence the constant upgrades. "Imperfections are really just profit opportunities waiting to be seized." ∎

pages that followed.

But all this was simply not enough. In the cramped converted garage which served as The Week's first office, half a mile from Paddington station, the bills pouring in drowned the meagre subscription cheques, and the steady whittling away of our limited funds soon began to exercise our office manager, Brigadier Clendon Daukes. Clendon was always cheerful and never made a fuss. In his previous job he had been responsible for distributing food to the Nato armies throughout the Balkans. But that was a doddle, he used to admit, compared with looking after The Week.

There were times I felt worried – and frustrated. What was wrong with people? Why couldn't they see how good The Week was?

In fact the response rates to our direct mail were a lot better than I believed they were – and it would soon be clear that almost nobody who subscribed would cancel. But none of this was much comfort at the time, especially as my expectations, like many another small businessman's, were far too high.

Three weeks after launching The Week I received a letter from a man I'd never heard of before: Felix Dennis. He congratulated me on launching The Week, said how much he liked it and suggested "sharing a beer". He had an ulterior motive, he admitted. He would be willing to invest, and to help.

"Anyone heard of Felix Dennis?" I asked, waving the letter about. No one had.

But it wasn't as if there were millionaires queuing round the block to invest in The Week and at this stage any avenue was worth exploring. So I set off to meet Felix in his flat in Soho. We were an odd couple, very different in many - though by no means all - ways. Felix, with his wild hair (even wilder than mine) talked energetically about his publishing business and about his new men's magazine, Maxim, his latest success, and about the American view - also his own - that direct mail marketing is not an art but a science. Think about my offer, he said as I was leaving. I will, I promised, and I did.

Back at Junction Mews, the bills continued to arrive. One evening I ran into John Brown at a literary party in the unlikely surroundings of 11 Downing Street. John was the publisher of Viz, and six months earlier I'd tried and failed to persuade him to take a stake in The Week.

"I've met this bloke called Felix Dennis," I said. "He wants to invest."

"He's perfect," said John. "He's got pots of money and he's particularly good at selling magazines by subscription, which is just what you need."

He was right. In his own account of our meeting in his book *How To Get Rich*, Felix writes that when he met me The Week was so underfunded that "the writing was on the wall. Without a big injection of cash it was all over." It's hard to disagree. Of all my failings in those early days, the greatest was to pay too much attention to editorial and too little to the business itself. Had I raised more money, had I put much more emphasis on the bottom line and had I hired an experienced publishing executive – Felix's first, and very sensible, piece of advice – we might have had a chance. As it was, I was like a man trying to hang pictures on the walls while a gale blows the roof off his house. I didn't have a hope.

Felix and I met for a second time under an oak tree in his garden near Stratford-upon-Avon – it was a hot summer, and a lot of business was done outside. I outlined a not very well thought out deal – on the back of an envelope, or possibly a cheque book – and in an equally cavalier way Felix agreed to it.

His finance director, Ian Leggett, a canny and diplomatic New Zealander, then came round to inspect the books. Ian doesn't much like deals done in gardens on the back of envelopes, but over the next few months he quietly made sense of it all. There was a price to be paid, of course – the heady feeling of being entirely on one's own was gone – but so were the anxieties, the living hand to mouth, the endless calculations over late night suppers as to how long we might last.

Felix said to me once that his secret is to know what other people want a moment before they do. He'd done it with kung fu magazines, and with computer magazines. He felt the same way about The Week. In the months that followed several rich businessmen rang me up, some, like Lord Hanson, because they were curious about The Week and wanted to inspect me as if I were some odd creature at a zoo, others to ask me why I hadn't come to them for money. The answer was that they weren't there when needed. Felix was. And with his help The Week soon began to prosper.

***

The idea for The Week came to me while walking in the hills near my family home in Pitlochry in Scotland in January 1994. My father had just died and I had started thinking seriously about the future.

Like many journalists, I'd long dreamt of breaking away on my own. But to do what?

There I was, deputy editor of The Sunday Telegraph, struggling across London every day from Brook Green to Canary Wharf, that eerie urban wilderness of concrete and glass, with, in those days, scarcely a pub or restaurant worthy of the name – purgatory for any journalist who, like me, enjoys a good West End lunch. I could see the years stretching ahead of sitting on the Docklands Light Railway.

In my job, like all newspaper executives, I spent a lot of time reading rival newspapers. It often occurred to me that however much I read I always seemed to miss at least one gem.

A year or two earlier I'd toyed with the idea of a specialist daily service for professionals, such as lawyers and doctors, finding stories relevant to them and sending these out by fax. Now I had a different idea. What about a digest of the week's news and comment, especially comment, highlighting the most arresting and original ideas, the funniest stories, the most interesting articles from abroad, the best houses on the market – everything I would like to know all together in one succinct, easy-to-read package? Most of the elements of The Week as it is now came to me on that walk.

My idea seemed even better given all the studies saying how busy we'd all become, working 16 hour days before learning Spanish or going white water rafting at weekends. There was a mismatch: longer and longer papers, less and less time to read them.

Women, in particular, I thought, would welcome such a digest. "Tell me what's going on," Alexandra, my wife, would say when we went out to dinner.

"Why not read a paper?"

"I don't have time."

Women lead much more interrupted lives than men and are usually busier, juggling several different roles and rarely getting more than 20 minutes at a stretch in which to read a paper. Women's arms are shorter too – and broadsheet newspapers are big and cumbersome and untidy.

The more I thought about it, the more sense my idea seemed to make: it couldn't be politically partisan, of course, but it would have to have an attitude, a personality, as all successful magazines

Early days at The Week

must have; a bland digest would never work.

Back at my mother's house I flicked through The Mail on Sunday and read an article defending fox hunting by John Mortimer – even then, it was a hot issue. As a trial, I grabbed a pen and paper and summarised it, including the odd quote. The end result came out at 190 words, roughly the length of the summaries on the *Best Articles* page in The Week.

I returned to London full of confidence, a confidence that was further boosted by a visit to a fortune teller in Putney called Mrs Peters. Mrs Peters consulted the tarot cards and pronounced that a door was about to close and that an opportunity was on the way, possibly helped by a big man with a booming voice (Felix?). She also told me it would make money which may have made me feel even more imprudent and impetuous than usual.

At any rate, a month later, convinced I wouldn't get anywhere unless I gave up my job, I went to see Charles Moore, The Sunday Telegraph editor, and resigned. He thought I was bonkers but was too polite, or too much of a friend, to say so.

As I worked out my notice I took advice from my friend Will Ellsworth Jones. Will was the chief reporter when I joined The Sunday Times in 1978 and helped me join the paper by holding my hand during a complicated investigation in Blackpool. Later I pestered him endlessly for advice while I was The Sunday Times Washington Correspondent in the mid 1980s.

Now he helped me again. He has a knack of identifying problems and knowing how to fix them and a very decided view of what works and what doesn't. He wasn't entirely convinced by my idea but did everything he could to assist in shaping it, encouraging among other things, the quirky side: it was he who suggested *Boring but important* and *It must be true, I read it in the tabloids.*

During the summer of 1994 I refined the editorial ideas. My hopeless sense of geography prompted the notion of using maps for foreign stories. Driving to buy some milk on the West Coast of Scotland in August, I thought up *All you need to know about everything that matters.* But I was stumped by what to call the magazine itself. I'd bored everyone with uninspired suggestions. One of these was The Weekly Digest. Finally I thought: why not lose the word digest? Just call it The Week.

By the time I left The Sunday Telegraph, in September, I'd made little progress in setting up a business. As well as throwing in my job, I'd persuaded Alexandra that we should sell our London house and move to Wiltshire with Ivar, our son, and our two girls, one, Ciara, a baby, the other, Flora, a four-year-old yanked unceremoniously from her London school and pitched into one in Calne. Several times a week I trailed in to London with a business plan saying I needed £1m, and talked to venture capitalists: it was a dispiriting few months. Venture capitalists are not well named. They were mildly curious and politely gave me their time but they didn't want to do much venturing. Their answer, in all cases, was no.

"It's the wrong sum of money you're after," said a businessman I know well. "Too small to interest the City, too big for your friends."

In the end, my breakthrough came at the prompting of an old television friend, Michael Wills, now a Labour peer, who put me in touch with an engaging media entrepreneur called John Gordon. Sitting in John's glass office in Islington looking out over a big room full of people at banks of computer screens I still wasn't entirely sure what his company, The Register Group, actually did – something to do with TV advertising – but whatever it was it felt very successful.

"You're going about this in the wrong way," he said. "Don't do it as a glossy magazine. Do it on subscription."

The distributors of magazines, he explained, take about 25% of the cover price while the newsagents take another 25%, meaning we'd only get half what we charged for each copy of The Week. There'd be a time lag of three months before we got our share of the money. And we'd never know how many magazines to print.

On the other hand, if we went the subscription route it would mean we wouldn't need to use expensive glossy paper and could design a publication more like a newsletter than a magazine – much cheaper – and, crucially, we would get a year's money from subscribers up front. "And go and see my friend Jeremy O'Grady. He's a bit idle but he's a good writer. He'll help you. And you won't have to pay him much." I took his advice - on all counts. I raised just under £200,00, half of it from the proceeds of our London house, half from friends and family, though this was a good deal less than what it took in the end to bring the magazine into profit.

And I went to find O'Grady in a Holland Park house almost impossible to enter because of the number of bicycles blocking the hall and took him out to lunch. Would he like a job, I wondered. He had just ended a spell as one of Britain's film censors, proved very congenial, quickly grasped the point of The Week and a month later, after Christmas, was helping me put together a dummy in John Gordon's office. Jeremy did indeed prove to be a good writer and his relaxed writing style – and, very important too, his non-Fleet Street perspective – proved highly influential in giving the magazine the right tone as it still does. But hiring him was a gamble.

So was the rest of my hiring. Fleet Street journalists were hardly clamoring to come aboard and who can blame them given what a dodgy enterprise it seemed, so I had to employ who I could. "You're hired entirely for your looks," I would say to the women, which, though a joke, had a grain of truth in it since in most cases I had only the sketchiest idea of what they were capable of.

"There was no such thing as an interview process," said Susanna Gross, who played a crucial role in the early days. "It was a quick lunch, did you like this person, and if you did they were hired." Which about sums it up. I was astonishingly lucky to end up with a small and talented team and one capable of producing a publication that is a lot harder to put together than it looks.

Unsurprisingly, there was the odd hiccup along the way. In the fairly early days we once managed to print the same map pages twice. Our readership was either so small or so tactful that no one remarked on it. In our first July I was driving down to Cornwall for a brief holiday when my mobile rang. It had already been an eventful journey – I had just finishing picking up our belongings from the A30 having somehow failed to secure a case properly on the roof rack. Now Jeremy rang to say that we'd misnamed The Duke of Westminster in our Desert Island Discs column and given him a profession he didn't have (designer), which was not what we wanted to do to one of our first subscribers. Our apology the next week got his name wrong again. Amazingly, despite this double incompetence, he continued to subscribe.

With our little team, and with Felix behind us, we began to grow steadily moving from 2,500 subscribers our first Christmas to around 12,000 a year later. Now it is more than ten times that and almost nothing, I'm happy to say, has had to be changed. The formula has proved a robust one and the magazine which rolls off the presses each week is pretty much the same as the one I picked up to examine on May 10, 1995.

A note on Connell Guides

Some of the quotes on previous pages come from Connell Guides (of which there are now more than 80). I have also quoted from interviews with William Boyd, Sebastian Faulks and Robert Harris. These are available on Youtube, as are videos of others who have helped me with the guides, including Helena Bonham Carter and Joanna Lumley (both choosing their favourite poems), Jonathan Bate talking about Shakespeare and John Mullan talking about Jane Austen.

On page 79 I have included some covers of Golf Quarterly, a magazine I started with Tim Dickson, its brilliant editor, more than a decade ago.

ℭℭ CONNELL GUIDES

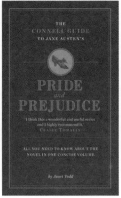

"The Connell Guides are brief, attractive, erudite, and to the point. Bravo!"
Sir Tom Stoppard

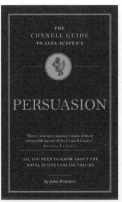

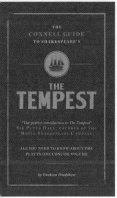

*"What I love about these is that they're small &
unintimidating, so they make the potentially
intimidating accessible"*
Helena Bonham Carter

ALL YOU NEED TO KNOW...

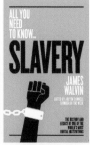
ALL YOU NEED TO KNOW...
SLAVERY
JAMES WALVIN
EDITED BY JOLYON CONNELL
FOUNDER OF THE WEEK
THE HISTORY AND LEGACY OF ONE OF THE WORLD'S MOST BRUTAL INSTITUTIONS

ALL YOU NEED TO KNOW...
THE BRITISH EMPIRE
HOW IT WAS BUILT AND HOW IT FELL
PIERS BRENDON
EDITED BY JOLYON CONNELL
FOUNDER OF THE WEEK

ALL YOU NEED TO KNOW...
WORLD WAR II
A BRILLIANT ACCOUNT OF THE MOST TERRIBLE EVENT IN HUMAN HISTORY
MAX HASTINGS
EDITED BY JOLYON CONNELL
FOUNDER OF THE WEEK

ALL YOU NEED TO KNOW...
THE AMERICAN CIVIL WAR
THE STORY THAT MOST UNDERSTANDS TO MAKE SENSE OF MODERN AMERICA
ADAM SMITH
EDITED BY JOLYON CONNELL
FOUNDER OF THE WEEK

ALL YOU NEED TO KNOW...
CHURCHILL
PAUL ADDISON
EDITED BY JOLYON CONNELL
FOUNDER OF THE WEEK
A BRILLIANTLY CONCISE ACCOUNT OF HISTORY'S MOST FAMOUS HERO

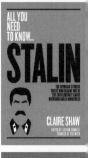
ALL YOU NEED TO KNOW...
STALIN
THE RUSSIAN STRONGMAN PRIEST WHO BECAME ONE OF THE 20TH CENTURY'S MURDEROUS MASS MURDERERS
CLAIRE SHAW
EDITED BY JOLYON CONNELL
FOUNDER OF THE WEEK

ALL YOU NEED TO KNOW...
THE AMERICAN REVOLUTION
WHY THE COLONISTS BROKE AWAY FROM BRITAIN AND FORGED A NEW NATION
STEPHEN CONWAY
EDITED BY JOLYON CONNELL
FOUNDER OF THE WEEK

ALL YOU NEED TO KNOW...
THE GREAT EXPLORERS
THE BRAVE ADVENTURERS WHO RISKED THEIR LIVES TO UNDERSTAND OUR OWN PLANET WORLD
ROBIN HANBURY TENISON
EDITED BY JOLYON CONNELL
FOUNDER OF THE WEEK

ALL YOU NEED TO KNOW...
HOW TO READ A POEM
A PRACTICAL GUIDE WHICH WILL OPEN YOUR EYES AND ENRICH YOUR HEART
MALCOLM HEBRON
EDITED BY JOLYON CONNELL
FOUNDER OF THE WEEK

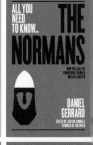
ALL YOU NEED TO KNOW...
THE NORMANS
HOW WILLIAM THE CONQUEROR CHANGED BRITAIN FOREVER
DANIEL GERRARD
EDITED BY JOLYON CONNELL
FOUNDER OF THE WEEK

ALL YOU NEED TO KNOW...
THE THIRD REICH
HOW WAS A BRUTAL DICTATORSHIP POSSIBLE IN A CIVILISED NATION IN THE MID 20TH CENTURY?
CAROLINE SHARPLES
EDITED BY JOLYON CONNELL
FOUNDER OF THE WEEK

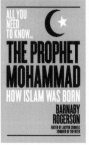
ALL YOU NEED TO KNOW...
THE PROPHET MOHAMMAD
HOW ISLAM WAS BORN
BARNABY ROGERSON
EDITED BY JOLYON CONNELL
FOUNDER OF THE WEEK

ALL YOU NEED TO KNOW...
WORLD WAR I
THE MOST CATASTROPHIC EVENT IN 20TH CENTURY EUROPEAN HISTORY
MAX EGREMONT
EDITED BY JOLYON CONNELL
FOUNDER OF THE WEEK

SHARPEN YOUR PEN WITH A LEADING EDITOR
ALL YOU NEED TO KNOW...
HOW TO WRITE WELL
TIM DE LISLE
EDITED BY JOLYON CONNELL
FOUNDER OF THE WEEK

Golf Quarterly

Elegant, witty writing on the game and its characters

Golf Quarterly

Playing for
high stakes

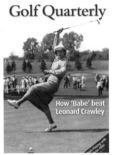

Golf Quarterly

How 'Babe' beat
Leonard Crawley

Golf Quarterly

My year as a
golf club captain

Golf Quarterly

The day Jack
lost his cool

Golf Quarterly

Temper
tantrums

Golf Quarterly

How good
a golfer is
Barack Obama?

Golf Quarterly

How the women's
game took off

Golf Quarterly

My round
with Donald
Trump

Golf Quarterly

Swinging sixties

First published in 2020 by Connell Publishing
Spye Arch House, Spye Park, Lacock WILTS SN15 2PR

10 9 8 7 6 5 4 3 2 1

A CIP catalogue record for this book is available from the British Library.
ISBN 978-1-911187-72-1

Designed and typeset by Paul Woodward

Printed in Great Britain

www.ConnellPublishing.com